Ifs, a Few Buts, and Other Stuff

Ifs, a Few Buts, and Other Stuff

Poems Mainly for Children by

Charles Hughes

Illustrations by

Beth Snider

Text copyright © 2024 Charles Hughes and
Illustrations copyright © 2024 Beth Snider. All rights reserved.
This material may not be reproduced in any form, published,
reprinted, recorded, performed, broadcast,
rewritten or redistributed without
the explicit permission of Charles Hughes and Beth Snider.
All such actions are strictly prohibited by law.

Cover design by Shay Culligan
Front and back cover images by Beth Snider
Author photo by Bunny Hughes

ISBN: 978-1-63980-661-4

Kelsay Books
502 South 1040 East, A-119
American Fork, Utah 84003
Kelsaybooks.com

*For Ellie, for Cy, for Zenia,
with love, with love, with love*

Acknowledgments

Grateful acknowledgment is made to the editors of the following publications, in which certain of these poems first appeared:

Amethyst Review: "But Then"
The Dirigible Balloon: "Be Careful If," "A Hard Lesson for King Midas," "If All the Stars," "If Not for Blue," "If Not for Combs," "If Not for Shoes"
Foreshadow: "A Ragged Man Comes to Dinner"
Lighten Up Online: "About My Future Phone," "If I Were Older"
The North American Anglican: "If You Begin"
Pure in Heart Stories: "But People Used to Be," "If Not for Light"
San Diego Reader: "If It Were March," "If You Had Been There"
THINK: "The Wild Horse"

And special thanks also to Beth Snider for her wonderful illustrations, without which this book would be much less. And to Michael Martin for his close reading, affirmation, and insights.

Contents

Summer Song	11
If All the Stars	13
But Who?	14
In a Summer Storm: A Riddle	16
If Not for Shoes	17
The Wild Horse	18
But and *Butt*	19
If It Were March	20
Climbing High: A Riddle	21
If You Had Been There	23
If Not for Clouds	24
Certain Things	25
A Ragged Man Comes to Dinner	27
Cases of Inside Places: A Riddle	32
A Hard Lesson for King Midas	33
But Then	34
If Not for Wind	35
Be Careful If	37
If Not for Combs	38
But People Used to Be	39
Looking Up: A Riddle	41
If You Begin	43
About My Future Phone	44
If Not for Light	45
Now That It's Fall	46
If Not for Presents	47
Once on a Summer Morning	49
Something in Common: A Riddle	51
If I Were Older	52
But Now	53
If Not for Grandfathers	55
If Not for Blue	56
If Stars Were All	57
Answers to Riddles	59

Summer Song

Soon the young sun will blossom and begin
To bring out children, grown-ups, walking in

Cool air, which won't stay cool for long.
They'll walk and sing a summer song,

Caroling the new day
In bloom along the way.

They'll hope that you
Will breathe it too

And share
This air.

If All the Stars

If all the stars were peppermints,
Then you could lie in bed
And breathe night air alive with hints
Of kindness overhead—

Fresh, cool, clean air from farther north
Than you have ever been,
From somewhere heavenlier than earth—
A sweeter oxygen—

And you might dream about a tree
You knew but now is gone,
A tree to swing on, climb, and be
A friend to until dawn.

But Who?

"It sounds like you were dreaming,"
My father answered, and
It's true I had been sleeping.
But who would understand?

Awake—but what awoke me?
A noise, I think, a thud.
I stood glued to my window
And stared out at the flood:

White light flowing like lava
From something on the ground,
A large bright beach ball, moonlike—
Faint eyes, nose, mouth that frowned—

The Moon!—but now no longer
Lighting the late-night skies—
Shrunk—fallen to Earth—still glowing.
Then came the real surprise:

The night sang out in voices,
All giggles—though, to me
A choir almost. I listened.
They laughed in harmony.

The laughter lasted only
Until a thunderous roar,
Which may well have been thunder—
Of that, I won't say more.

Who says we can't hear angels
Or that they never stretch
A point (as any child might)
To play a game of catch?

The Moon was gone next morning,
Soon back in its old place,
From which it shone next evening.
It didn't leave a trace.

In a Summer Storm: A Riddle

Loud booms and bangs and rain downpouring,
Fireworks in the dark sky.
Without a raincoat or umbrella,
You're far from dry.

Wind lashes trees, bending strong branches.
You feel a couple of stings
From pea-sized pearls of ice, now missiles—
What are these things?

If Not for Shoes

If not for shoes,

Your feet would balk,

Resist, refuse

To run or walk

On ice and snow

Or anywhere

Even one toe

Might freeze if bare.

Socks try, although

Feet mostly find

That socks do less

And can't be shined

Without a mess.

The Wild Horse

Imagine a wild horse
You dreamt, then painted. See him run
Through rain and wind, a storm that's getting worse.
The painting isn't done.

More lightning high above
The darkening canyon casts a glare
On giant rocks and flowing puddles of
Rainwater everywhere.

The horse runs, almost flies.
His hooves don't touch the canyon floor.
You use the lightning color for his eyes
And paint his chest a blur

Of oddly bright spring green,
A color no real horse could be.
Horses don't come in greens, although you've seen
A green horse recently,

Much too alive to lose.
You paint the headlong way he runs.
Like spring, the horse brings beauty and good news,
Being both of these at once.

But and *Butt*

Two words he loved and used—
A certain boy in second grade—
Not that he got confused—
The dictionary had okayed

Them both. He'd checked, and he
Would calmly, if rebuked, intone,
"I'm saying *B-U-T,*
Which is what's called a homophone."

If It Were March

If it were March—say, early March—a day
Much more like late-June days, the sun
Warm, waking up as if to say,
"Spring's off, summer's begun!"—

Which would, with spring in the wings, be out of whack,
A little premature as yet—
Your thoughts might leap ahead, then back
To days you won't forget.

You might remember summer words, might find
Words hidden away since winter's start
Returning now—words called to mind
For things you know by heart:

Lake, woods, dark nights, bright stars, breeze in tall trees,
Beach, raft, steep slide, sand, picnic, ants.
The mind replays good memories
If given half a chance.

Climbing High: A Riddle

Nothing but ice and snow,
Cold, hard-to-breathe thin air.
As far as people know,
They were the first ones there:

In 1953,
With Tenzing Norgay, his guide,
Sir Edmund Hillary
Achieved what others had tried.

For reaching its full height,
The two of them won fame
And accolades. You might—
Or do you?—know its name.

If You Had Been There

> The famous appearance of a boy and girl—a very long time ago, in the Village of Woolpit, in Suffolk, England—both of them wearing unfamiliar clothing and speaking an unknown language, both with green skin—has never been fully explained.

If you had been there on the day

The two green children first appeared,

What do you think you would have done?

A priest might have knelt down to pray.

A doctor might have looked up weird

Diseases, then advised more sun.

You would have been more practical,

Knowing the world a child knows,

The frightened children's quiet mood,

That it's a hard thing, feeling small

And strange and far from home. Clean clothes,

Warm smile, warm place to sleep, some food—

You would, at least, have offered these,

Knowing they're all necessities.

If Not for Clouds

If not for clouds, the sky
Would lose its old allure.
The sun would make us cry;
Its light would be too pure.

We'd wish for medium grays,
The restfulness, the cool
Of soothing rainy days.
Straight sunshine would be cruel.

But look! Clouds decorate
The heavens—they're still here:
Thin, wispy ones and great
White towers. Our atmosphere

Knits up the beauties of
The sun, the clouds, the air
To fit us like a glove.
We don't have clouds to spare.

Certain Things

Who doesn't stop to think about
Certain things truly lost for good?
Your fact-filled book of rainbow trout,
In which bugs show up, too, as food—

Maybe? Or maybe that gold pair
Of cufflinks from Great Uncle Paul
You weren't at first sure how to wear.
Or those old playing cards with all

The Smoky Mountains standing on
Their backs, a childhood souvenir—
A father's, passed down to his son.

Some things we lose we don't hold dear
And don't remember. Others, though,
We love and lose and can't let go.

A Ragged Man Comes to Dinner

(a poem in three parts)

Part One

Two children and two parents
Moved from a house they loved,
Which made the children angry
Much as when you've been shoved.

Their new house had stood empty,
A long, long way from new.
The roof leaked, so they fixed it.
Rain kept on leaking through.

A field of grass stretched, hilly,
Behind the house. A hill—
The children, summer evenings,
Would go if possible.

Katie brought chalks and paper
For pictures sunsets made.
Nathaniel, picturing treasure,
Dug holes with an old spade.

Something about those evenings—
Maybe the soil and sky?
The children's anger faded.
They couldn't have said why.

One evening as clouds colored,
Cloud whites to rose-pink smears,
And piles of dirt grew taller,
Slow footsteps jarred their ears.

A limping man paused, struggling
Unsteadily to stand.
Katie—protective, older—
Reached for Nathaniel's hand.

Part Two

The children weren't that frightened.
They'd seen such men before.
The year was 1930:
Hard times; there'd been the war.

"That brown house," Katie pointed.
"The church just down the way—
Our father's the new pastor.
We . . . Oh! Are you okay?"

The man, standing but teetering,
Fell to one knee, knelt, then
After a moment, managed
To stand—wobbly—again.

His clothes old, frayed—eyes staring
As if he'd seen a ghost—
"I'm searching for a relic
From the war," he said, "it's lost—

"A barbed-wire cross—in ribbon—
Crimson—laced, sewn in place—
Too fine for my jacket pocket."
Tears glistened on his face.

"A friend died who had made it,"
He told them, looking where
Nathaniel stooped low, digging.
The cross was buried there.

Both children watched him limping,
Going back the way he'd come,
Until the twilight hid him.
The children started home.

Part Three

The man sat at the table.
A Sunday dinner. Rain
Outside dripped from the ceiling.
He ate and tried to explain.

Nathaniel elbowed Katie.
No reason. He was bored.
Their mother glared a warning.
Patience, she prayed to the Lord.

The man, more ragged, hungry—
But answering what he could—
Spoke of the war, the sadness,
The beauty of the food.

Cases of Inside Places: A Riddle

Snug homes for bats, for ancient humans, for
Hermits, who only want to be alone.
Hideouts where thieves can steal away and store
Valuables—other people's, not their own.
Elijah found he couldn't stay in one,
And Tom and Becky finally find their way
Back out. What places don't much feel the sun,
Are always filled with night and never day?

A Hard Lesson for King Midas

Nobody wishes now
To be King Midas, who,
By wishing, showed us how
Wishes can come too true,

Can court catastrophe.
King Midas asked too much.
He wished and instantly
Was given the golden touch,

Which meant he turned whatever
He touched, including food,
Into gold. (Metal should never—
No matter what!—be chewed.)

King Midas found a cure
For this once-wished-for curse—
Luckily, since things were
Headed from bad to worse.

But Then

In times long past, you would have known
The wind, the birds, and how
Birds have a calling like your own.
You may not know this now.

The wind blows where it wills, we're told;
Birds neither sow nor reap—
They sing into the wind their old
Songs that still laugh or weep.

But, then, you would have understood—
Have felt—their songs as prayer,
As happy or sad, as beauty and good,
As love filling the air.

If Not for Wind

If not for wind, you'd look
Up into pale blue air
And see the same old clouds unshook,
Unchanging, always there

Morning to afternoon,
Each boringly still day.
You'd feel wrapped tight in a cocoon
And yearn to get away,

Back to where wind keeps blowing
And clouds stay on the move—
Gusts blustering, coming and going,
You'd miss but do not love.

Be Careful If

Be very careful if you find
That creatures you draw, once you've put down
Your crayon, pencil or pen, become
Real, living beings—the breathing kind:
Lions, let's say, all tawny brown,
Suddenly there, on the attack,
Hungry, life size, roaring, just some
Inches from where you're sitting. Run!
Or instead, try yellow Labs. Draw one,
Whose chestnut eyes outlined in black
See only you—who'll love you back.

If Not for Combs

If not for combs, what would become of hair?
There will be those who answer, "We don't care!"

They'll say, "We like our hair uncombed and wild.
We let it stand or fall or intertwine—
Whatever—just so long as it's unstyled.
What plant outshines a free, untrellised vine?"

Well, yes, I see their point, but I've long known
My hair's not at its best when on its own.

But People Used to Be

"Jump back!" she heard, and she jumped back.
(This happened long ago.)
A lightning flash, then thunder. Crack!
The tree just missed her toe.

Her father said she shouldn't have
Gone outside in the storm.
Her mother rubbed some smelly salve
On scratches on her arm.

Her brother felt and didn't see
The hand that stopped him short,
Feet from a snake coiled patiently,
Poisonous in the dirt.

"There are," their grandmother would say,
"Guardian angels, who
Try to protect us night and day,
As yours protected you."

But people used to be more sure
Of angels within reach,
Blessings the children's grandmother
Took every chance to teach.

Looking Up: A Riddle

Certain beauty travels vast
Distances through time and space,
From an eon eons past,
Unexhausted, still ablaze.

Elevate your eyes, but choose
When and where. Then you will see
Tapestries of—what? Some clues:
Bonfires burning countlessly;

Sunlight keeps them out of sight;
Other lights can hide them, too;
Best to look on a dark night;
Darkness brings them into view.

If You Begin

If you begin a lullaby,
You'll know what words, what tune.
The harder question, though, is *why*,
Which—like a red balloon

Floating along, as evening comes,
On soft, pale purple air,
Just out of reach of laws and sums,
Unanswered—hovers there.

The red balloon floats there alone,
Dark seeping in from shade.
No wonder we're so often prone
To go to bed afraid.

This *why*, I hope, won't trouble you;
With patience, questions keep.
It certainly won't matter to
The one you sing to sleep.

About My Future Phone

Ringtones, I've noticed, rarely ring,

Which seems a slightly phony thing.

The phone I plan to buy someday

Won't be the kind designed to play

Or sing a song to let me know

A call is coming in—oh, no!

Nor will it be so retro as

To ring like old phones no one has.

A quiet voice will do just fine,

Announcing who is on the line.

Unsadly, ringtone, as a word,

Soon could be turned way down, unheard.

If Not for Light

If not for light, the darkness
Would cover all that is.
Just think of the awful chaos—
No, wait! Don't think of this!

Better instead to remember,
When you can't help but see
Darkness in every corner
Advancing steadily

To cover you—remember
God's love made all that is
And won't permit the darkness
To cover up what's his.

Remember in the beginning,
How nothing had begun,
Until God lit the darkness?
Light came before the sun.

Now That It's Fall

The breeze has gone from warm to cool
And soon will blow much colder.
As usual, I'm back in school,
The usual year older.

My grandpa wants the warmth to last,
Summer to keep repeating.
Summer, he says, goes way too fast.
I get it—time is fleeting,

And winter waits impatiently;
The season is always turning.
Fall will fly by but stay with me:
I've seen the fall fires burning.

If Not for Presents

If not for presents, I would be
Happy but in a sadder way.
Birthdays come so infrequently,
And when they finally do, don't stay
For long. Why not appreciate
The benefits of turning eight?
Or any age? Between the two,
Receiving's certainly less blessed
Than giving, but it's also true
That birthdays will be at their best
When presents mix with partying,
Making a happy birthday sing.

Once on a Summer Morning

Robert, first thing, got dressed, went out.
He looked up toward the sun,
Already blazing hot, about
As high as treetops run.

Robert kept looking up as if
Waiting but unaware
What for. Before too long, a whiff
Of sweetness tinged the air,

The musty river, morning heat,
Their scent he'd come to know;
A cardinal, landing at his feet,
Put on a silent show.

The cardinal danced without a sound,
Flew twenty feet away,
Then danced some more there on the ground,
Trying its best to say,

"Follow." So Robert followed as
The cardinal flew ahead,
Staying in Robert's sight because
Of how its reddest red

Flashed in the sunlit sky like flame,
A spark against bright blue.
One block, another block—they came
To where tall crabgrass grew

Along the riverbank, a place
Where Robert spent spare hours,
Watching the river's changing face
Or fashioning mud towers,

Which now his eyes searched for until
They glimpsed, in a shallow hole,
A turtle, upside down, stock-still,
A bowl stuck in a bowl.

Snapping? He paused. He used a stick
To flip the turtle over.
The turtle, free, discovered thick,
Inviting clumps of clover

And took to eating. That was when
Robert looked up to see
A small red flame in flight again . . .
Smaller . . . soon memory.

Something in Common: A Riddle

Great Britain is a famous one,
Also Tahiti and
Elba (from which Napoleon
Escaped for his last stand).

Notice the similarity
Geography presents.
What single word describes all three?
It isn't *continents*.

If I Were Older

If only I were older,
I'd speak a foreign tongue.
This would surprise my parents.
They'd wish that I were young.

Probably French, I'm thinking—
The Little Prince is why:
It's a grown-up Frenchman's story
That ends with a sad goodbye.

He may have been a grown-up,
But still he understood
How children see much better
What in the world is good.

Most grown-ups are too busy
To understand this quite.
Someday I'll tell my parents
In French, and I'll be right.

But Now

The weather's hot—
An August day—
So hot it's not
Much fun to play
Outdoors, until
The slightest breeze,
The faintest chill
Stir in the trees
Like melodies
As they arrive.
No time to mope!
It's ninety-five,
But now there's hope.

If Not for Grandfathers

If not for grandfathers, what then?
Whereas I know my grandchildren,
My grandfathers I never knew.
I'm at a loss to tell you who
They were—what kind of men—or why
I peer so hard through my mind's eye
To see behind their pictures, see
Them whole as though by memory.

If Not for Blue

If not for blue, then Earth might be
Some noisy color standing out
Among the planets like a shout
That wakes a napping nursery:

Blaring magenta, sharp chartreuse,
Shrill, brilliant white too bright to fade,
Hot pink in the most piercing shade,
Some color Mozart wouldn't choose.

Smaller things to consider: eyes,
Blueberries, Lake Lucerne. Why do
People adore the color blue?
Its peaceful tones—they're what we prize.

If Stars Were All

a poem for Epiphany

If stars were all
That we could see—
Their history—
That miracle—
How night and day,
Stars keep on shining,
By light defining
Love's constant way—

We might, then, dare
To trust much more
In love than war:
A Christmas prayer
The angels sing,
Stars brightening.

Answers to Riddles

"In a Summer Storm": hail

"Climbing High": Mount Everest

"Cases of Inside Places": caves

"Looking Up": stars

"Something in Common": islands

About the Author

Charles Hughes has published two previous books of poems, *The Evening Sky* and *Cave Art,* both from Wiseblood Books. His poems have appeared in various journals and magazines and are included in the anthologies, *Taking Root in the Heart* from Paraclete Press and *An Outcast Age* from Little Gidding Press. This is his first book of poems for children. He worked for over 30 years as a lawyer and lives in the Chicago area with his wife.

About the Illustrator

Beth Snider has illustrated more than twenty children's books, including several books in the "Variety Tales" series, created for Variety KC (a nonprofit for kids with disabilities), and the multi-award winning *Fly High: Understanding Grief with God's Help.* She lives near Kansas City, Kansas with her husband, four children, and black Lab.

www.ingramcontent.com/pod-product-compliance
Lightning Source LLC
Chambersburg PA
CBHW030915170426
43193CB00009BA/860